W9-CLV-417

# Body Fuel for Healthy Bodies
## Fats and Oils

Trisha Sertori

**Marshall Cavendish**
Benchmark

New York

This edition first published in 2009 in the United States of America by Marshall Cavendish Benchmark.

Marshall Cavendish Benchmark
99 White Plains Road
Tarrytown, NY 10591
www.marshallcavendish.us

First published in 2008 by
macmillan education australia pty ltd
15–19 Claremont Street, South Yarra 3141

Visit our website at www.macmillan.com.au or go directly to www.macmillanlibrary.com.au

Associated companies and representatives throughout the world.

Copyright © Macmillan Education Australia 2008

Library of Congress Cataloging-in-Publication Data

Sertori, Trisha.
    Fats and oils / by Trisha Sertori.
        p. cm. — (Body fuel for healthy bodies)
    Includes index.
    ISBN 978-0-7614-3798-7
    1. Lipids in human nutrition—Juvenile literature.  I. Title.
    QP751.S37 2009
    612.3'97—dc22

                                    2008026208


Edited by Margaret Maher
Text and cover design by Stella Vassiliou
Page layout by Stella Vassiliou
Photo research by Claire Francis
Illustrations by Toby Quarmby, Vishus Productions, pp. 4, 5; Jeff Lang and
    Stella Vassiliou, pp. 8, 9, 10; Stella Vassiliou pp. 22–23.

Printed in the United States

**Acknowledgments**
The author and publishers are grateful to the following for permission to reproduce copyright material:

Cover and header photos courtesy of © iStockphoto.com (oil & vinegar); © iStockphoto.com/Agisilaou & Spyrou (avocado); © iStockphoto.com/ Galina Barskaya (girl); © iStockphoto.com/Olga Lyubkina (bottle oil); © iStockphoto.com/Kristian Sekulic (boy); © iStockphoto.com/Vasiliki Varvaki (olives); © iStockphoto.com/Jaroslaw Wojcik (rosemary).

Photos courtesy of:
123RF/Heng Kong Chen, **28** (middle); BananaStock, **15** (bottom); © Aberenyi/Dreamstime.com, **26** (left); © Marcin Balcerzak/Dreamstime.com, **19** (top right); © Elena Elisseeva/Dreamstime.com, **20**; © Petr Jilek/Dreamstime.com, **7** (2nd bottom); © Daniela Spyropoulo/Dreamstime.com, **18**; © Emilia Stasiak/Dreamstime.com, **22** (oil bottle), **29** (3rd bottom right); Getty Images/Image Source, **12**; Getty Images/David Murray, **28** (2nd top); Getty Images/Purestock, **30**; Getty Images/Michael Rosenfeld, **7** (2nd top); Getty Images/Ted Thai, **25** (left); © iStockphoto.com, **16** (donuts & bottle), **28** (top & bottom), **29** (middle left, top right & 3rd top right); © iStockphoto.com/Jose Antonio Nicoli Andonie, **24** (top); © iStockphoto.com/Michael Blackburn, **11** (bottom); © iStockphoto.com/Vera Bogaerts, **14** (top), **22** (top); © iStockphoto.com/Robert Byron, **24** (bottom); © iStockphoto.com/Sandra Caldwell, **29** (2nd bottom right); © iStockphoto.com/Joe Gough, **7** (bottom); © iStockphoto.com/Timothy Large, **29** (2nd top right); © iStockphoto.com/Arturo Limon, **7** (top); © iStockphoto.com/Meg Lipscombe, **23** (top); © iStockphoto.com/Sean Locke, **27** (bottom); © iStockphoto.com/Vasko Miokovic, **17** (bottom); © iStockphoto.com/Martina Misar, **22** (middle); © iStockphoto.com/Amy Myers, **21** (bottom); © iStockphoto.com/Diane Rutt, **6** (top); © iStockphoto.com/Roman Sigaev, **29** (bottom right); © iStockphoto.com/Suzannah Skelton, **16** (olives), **29** (middle right); © iStockphoto.com/Vasiliki Varvaki, **1**, **3**; © 2008 Jupiterimages, **6** (bottom); MEA Photos/Lesya Bryndzia, **29** (top left); Photolibrary/John Bavosi/ Science Photo Library, **13** (left); Photolibrary/Anthony Blake Photolibrary, **25** (right); Photolibrary/Food Alan King/Alamy, **22** (seeds); Photolibrary/ Philippe Psaila/Science Photo Library, **11** (top); Photolibrary/Richard Wadey/Alamy, **19** (top left); Photolibrary © A.T. Willett/Alamy, **26** (right); Photos.com, **16** (avocado); Trisha Sertori, **23** (bottom), **23** (middle); © Rafa Irusta/Shutterstock, **28** (2nd bottom); © Susan Kehoe/Shutterstock, **14** (bottom); © Christopher Meder/Shutterstock, **8**, **9** (bottom), **10**; © Shapiso/Shutterstock, **16** (seeds).

MyPyramid symbols courtesy of U.S. Department of Agriculture.

While every care has been taken to trace and acknowledge copyright, the publisher tenders their apologies for any accidental infringement where copyright has proved untraceable. Where the attempt has been unsuccessful, the publisher welcomes information that would redress the situation.

1  3  5  6  4  2

# Contents

## Glossary Words

When a word is printed in **bold**, you can look up its meaning in the Glossary on page 31.

# What Is Body Fuel?

Body fuel is the energy, vitamins, and minerals we need to live. Just as cars need gasoline and computers need electricity, people need energy, vitamins, and minerals to work.

The best way to fuel our bodies is with a **balanced diet**. A balanced diet gives us all the **nutrients** our bodies need.

## Nutrients in Foods

The nutrients in foods are divided into macronutrients and micronutrients.

Macronutrients provide energy. They are proteins, carbohydrates, and fats and oils. Micronutrients help **chemical reactions** take place in the body. They are vitamins and minerals.

## The Food Pyramid

The food pyramid lists foods for healthy bodies. The colors shown (from left to right) are for grains, vegetables, fruit, oils, dairy, and meat and beans.

MyPyramid.gov
STEPS TO A HEALTHIER YOU

## Fats and Oils

Fats and oils are macronutrients. This means they provide energy, or body fuel. Oils and fats have the most body fuel per ounce or per gram of all the macronutrients. However, they are also the least efficient form of energy.

Our bodies need some fats and oils daily, but only in very small amounts. Extra energy from fats and oils is stored as body fat. Too much body fat is unhealthy for our **internal organs**.

There are many different types of fats and oils. Some of these are healthy and some are unhealthy.

### Where On the Food Pyramid Are Fats and Oils?

Fats and oils are in the yellow part of the food pyramid. People should only eat small amounts.

**Fabulous Body Fuel Fact**

Exercise is the best way to burn extra fat. It is good for people in lots of other ways, too!

## Oils
### Know your Fats
MyPyramid.gov

# What Types of Fats and Oils Are There?

Fats and oils come from animal products, grains, fruits, and vegetables. Animal fats are saturated fats and are solid at room temperature. Oils from olives and avocados are mono-unsaturated oils. They are liquid at room temperature, but become solid in the refrigerator. Oils from grains and seeds are polyunsaturated oils. They stay liquid in all temperatures.

Polyunsaturated and mono-unsaturated oils are the healthiest of all fats and oils.

**Butter**
Butter is a saturated fat made from cow's milk. Cream from milk is **churned** until a watery liquid called buttermilk separates from the cream, leaving solid butter.

**Margarine**
Margarine is made from different types of polyunsaturated or mono-unsaturated oils. The oil is **hydrogenated** to make it look like butter, and to allow it to stay solid at room temperature. Some margarine can contain trans fats.

## Body Fuel Health Tips

There is a fourth category of fats called trans fats. These are polyunsaturated oils that have been hydrogenated. Trans fats affect the body in the same way as saturated fats.

## Polyunsaturated Oils

Polyunsaturated oils are produced from different grains, nuts, and legumes. These include walnuts, peanuts, safflowers and sunflowers, sesame seeds, soybeans, and corn.

## Saturated Fats from Plants

Palm and coconut oils are saturated fats from plants. Sawit palms are grown throughout Malaysia and Indonesia for palm oil. Coconut plantations in Fiji and Samoa produce coconut oil. This oil is liquid at room temperature, but becomes solid when chilled.

## Mono-unsaturated Oils

Mono-unsaturated oils are found in olives, avocados, canola, cashews, and almonds.

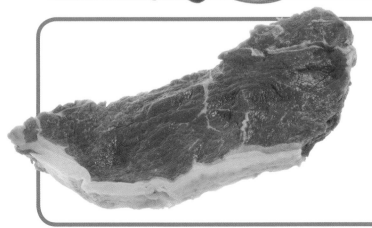

## Lard

Lard is the white saturated fat found on meats such as steak and pork. Lard melts off fatty meat during cooking and hardens as it cools. It is used in some countries to fry foods and make pastries.

# The Digestive System

The digestive system breaks down the foods we eat so they are ready to be absorbed into the bloodstream. Each part of the digestive system plays a part in breaking down, or digesting, foods. **Saliva** and **digestive enzymes** prepare to digest foods even before we eat them. They are produced when we see or smell foods.

### Mouth
Teeth cut and grind food into smaller pieces. The enzymes in saliva start to break down carbohydrates in the food. The chewed food becomes a **bolus**, which is pushed down the throat by the tongue when we swallow.

### Esophagus
The bolus travels down the esophagus (ee-*soff*-a-gus) to the stomach.

### Liver
The liver filters nutrients from the blood. Nutrients are sent to the small intestine for digestion. Waste is sent to the large intestine.

### Gallbladder
The gallbladder stores bile, which is a digestive liquid made by the liver. Bile is used in the small intestine to break down fats.

### Pancreas
The pancreas makes enzymes that break down macronutrients.

### Small Intestine
The small intestine is almost 23 feet (7 meters) long. Foods are digested in the small intestine after they are broken down in the stomach. Most nutrients are absorbed into our bloodstream through **villi** in the small intestine.

### Large Intestine
The large intestine is 5 feet (1.5 meters) long. It carries waste to the **rectum** for **evacuation** as **feces** (*fee*-seas).

### Stomach
Stomach muscles churn the bolus. Acid in the stomach makes the food watery.

## Fabulous Body Fuel Fact

A bolus takes about three seconds to reach your stomach after it is swallowed.

# How Does the Body Digest Fats and Oils?

Fats and oils are digested in the stomach and small intestine.

## The Stomach

In the stomach, fats and oils are churned up by the stomach muscles and broken into smaller pieces. This makes it easier for them to be digested in the small intestine.

## The Small Intestine and Pancreas

The pancreas sends a special enzyme called pancreatic lipase ( *pan*-kree-*at*-tic lie-pays) to the small intestine. In the small intestine, the pancreatic lipase breaks down fats so they can be absorbed into the bloodstream.

The pancreas makes enzymes that are sent to the small intestine to digest food.

### Fabulous Body Fuel Fact

Oils keep our skin waterproof and fats cushion us when we bump into something.

## Body Fuel Health Tips

An important role of fats is transporting the fat-soluble vitamins, A, D, E, and K. The body needs only a tiny amount of fat to do this job. **Fat-soluble vitamins** are stored in the liver for a long time.

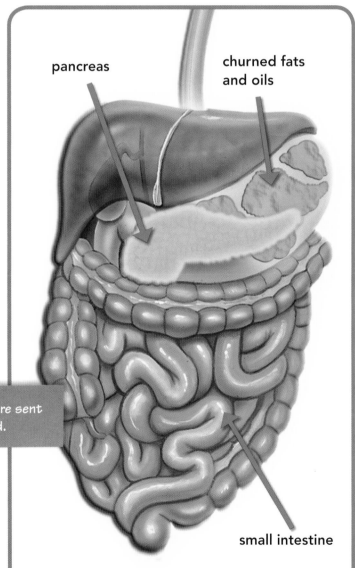

pancreas

churned fats and oils

small intestine

# How Does the Digestive System Absorb Fats and Oils?

Fats and oils are absorbed through villi in the small intestine. They are released into the bloodstream as blobs of digested fat.

## The Liver

The fatty blobs travel from the bloodstream through the liver. The liver removes wastes and stores fat-soluble vitamins. Some fats then travel to the large intestine as waste. Others travel through the **lymphatic system**.

The liver controls fat release into **cells** and organs. It also controls bile. Bile is stored in the gallbladder. It breaks up fats in the small intestine, like detergent working on greasy plates.

## The Small Intestine

The broken-up fats are absorbed into the cells of the small intestine. Inside these cells, the fats are broken up even more, and then packaged with proteins to make fatty blobs called lipoproteins (*lie*-poe-proteins). The body produces an enzyme called lipoprotein lipase to chop the fats up again. This makes them tiny enough to enter other cells in the body.

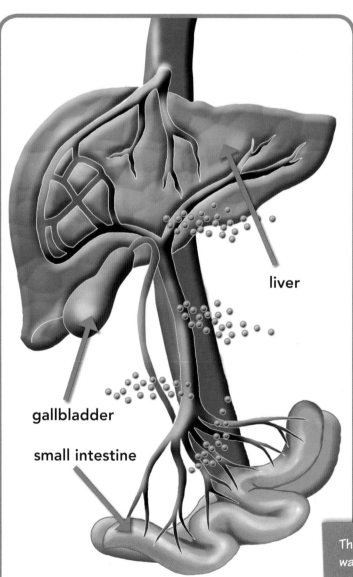

liver

gallbladder

small intestine

The liver acts as a filter to remove waste from the blood.

# How Do Fats and Oils Help the Body Function?

Fats are used throughout the body by cells, **hormones**, and the brain.

## Cells

Cells have thin skins, called membranes, which let nutrients into the cells. Without nutrients, cells cannot function properly. Fats and oils keep cell membranes flexible so nutrients can enter and waste can be removed.

The best oils for cell membranes are polyunsaturated and mono-unsaturated oils. Cells use tiny amounts of saturated fats, produced by the body. Excess saturated fats make cell membranes sticky and inflexible.

## Hormones

Many hormones depend on fats and oils for transport throughout the body.

## The Brain

The best fats for brain function are fats from fish. These fats are similar to the fats that form the brain.

Cells are tightly packed together to make up all the parts of the body.

Fish contains healthy fats, such as omega-3 fatty acids.

Fats and oils are macronutrients. They provide the most energy per ounce (or per gram) of any macronutrient. Fats and oils have some of the fat-soluble vitamins A, D, and E. More important, fats and oils have essential fatty acids called omega-6 fatty acid and omega-3 fatty acid. The body can make all the other essential fats it needs from these two essential fats.

| Nutrients in Fats and Oils | | | | | |
|---|---|---|---|---|---|
| Nutrients | Butter | Margarine (Often Fortified with Vitamins) | Lard | Mono-unsaturated Fats, such as Olive Oil | Polyunsaturated Fats, such as Sunflower Oil |
| **Vitamins** | | | | | |
| vitamin A | • | • | | | |
| vitamin B1 | | • | • | | |
| vitamin B2 | | • | • | | |
| vitamin D | • | • | | | |
| vitamin E | | • | | | |
| **Minerals** | | | | | |
| iron | | | • | | |
| zinc | | | • | | |
| potassium | | | • | | |
| magnesium | | | • | | |
| **Fatty Acids** | | | | | |
| linolenic acid | | | • | | |
| myristoleic acid | | | • | • | |
| oleic fatty acid | | | | • | |
| omega-3 fatty acid | • | | | • | • |
| omega-6 fatty acid | | | • | | • |
| palmitoleic acid | | | | • | |

Fats and oils from different sources contain different micronutrients and fatty acids.

**Bones**
Vitamin D and vitamin K are used for healthy bone formation and bone strength.

# How Does the Body Use These Nutrients?

The body needs some fat for healthy cell membranes, brain function, and to transport fat-soluble vitamins and minerals throughout the body. Vitamins are used in the body in different ways. Fats and oils also have fatty acids called omega-3 and omega-6.

**Brain**
Omega-3 and omega-6 fatty acids promote healthy brain function.

**Blood**
Vitamin E helps produce red blood cells. Vitamin K is used in blood **clotting**. It may help slow the body's aging process, and it assists in human growth.

**Heart and Lungs**
Vitamin A is an **antioxidant** and is used in heart and lung health.

**Liver**
The liver stores the fat-soluble vitamins A, D, E, and K. If people eat lots of foods that are high in fat-soluble vitamins, they can get sick. This is called a vitamin overdose.

**Skin and Cell Membranes**
Omega-3 and omega-6 fatty acids help make the skin waterproof and keep cell membranes flexible.

**Immune System**
Vitamin A strengthens the **immune system.**

## Fabulous Body Fuel Fact

Too much vitamin A from foods such as carrots turns feet and palms orange!

# Fueling the Body with Fats and Oils

The energy in foods comes originally from the Sun. Plants absorb energy from sunlight. Animals gain this energy when they graze on plants. When people eat foods from plants and animals, they are eating the sunlight energy. Fats and oils have large amounts of stored sunlight energy.

## Measuring Energy

Energy is measured in kilojoules. Most adults need between 1,800 to 2,800 calories (7,500–11,500 kilojoules) of energy daily.

Fats and oils have 9 cal (37 kJ) of energy per 1 gram. That is more than twice as much as carbohydrate foods.

The daily energy people get from fats should be less than 480 cal (2,000 kJ). Most foods naturally contain some fats. These fats need to be counted in the daily fat intake.

When sheep eat plants, such as grass, they absorb the energy stored in the plants.

### Fabulous Body Fuel Fact

Some animals sleep, or hibernate, throughout winter. Bears that hibernate eat enough food to double their weight during the fall. During hibernation, this stored fat keeps the bears alive.

Bears use their fat as body fuel so they can sleep through the winter.

# How Much Energy from Fats and Oils Is Needed Each Day?

People need between two and four tablespoons of fat daily. Much of this fat is already in foods. Only tiny amounts of added fat are needed.

## Polyunsaturated Fats

Polyunsaturated fats come from plants and fish. They contain essential omega-3 and omega-6 fatty acids. Polyunsaturated fats are good for people because the body cannot make these fatty acids.

## Mono-unsaturated Fats

People do not need mono-unsaturated fats in the diet because the body makes this fat. However, mono-unsaturated fats, such as olive oil, are much healthier than saturated fats. Mono-unsaturated oils may also be good for the heart.

## Saturated Fats

People do not need any saturated fats in the diet, since the body makes this fat. Foods such as doughnuts, pastries, cakes, chocolates, sausages, and salami are high in saturated fats. They should be eaten sparingly.

*Body Fuel Health Tips*

Adolescent boys age ten to twelve doing moderate exercise need about 1,800 to 2,200 cal (7,500–9,500 kJ) of energy daily. Girls the same age need a bit less, about 1,800 to 2,000 cal (7,500–8,500 kJ).

People need only small amounts of fat, so lean meat is a healthy food to choose.

# Healthy Food Choices

Some food choices are healthier than others. Polyunsaturated oils are the healthiest choice in fats and oils. Replace saturated fats with polyunsaturated or mono-unsaturated fats for an easy healthy food choice. The following table shows some healthy ways to prepare and eat fats and oils.

| ✔ Healthiest Choices | ✔ Healthy Choices | ✗ Less Healthy Choices |
|---|---|---|
| salad dressings made with polyunsaturated oil | canola oil | doughnuts |
| safflower oil | avocados | pastries made with butter |
| sunflower oil | olive oil | chocolate |
| sesame oil | | foods deep-fried in saturated fat |
| flaxseed oil | | butter |
| fish oils | | cakes |
| peanut oil | | cookies |
| soybean oil | | sausages |

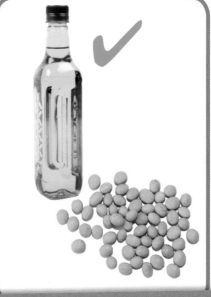

Choose oils from soybeans, avocados, and olives instead of foods with saturated fats, such as doughnuts.

## Trans Fats

Trans fats are chemically made fats that have had the gas hydrogen added to them. This makes them like a saturated fat. Trans fats are often used in manufactured foods, such as cakes and chocolates.

Trans fats may cause illnesses, including cancer and heart disease. Because of this, food labels in some countries, such as the United States list trans fats in foods.

### Fabulous Body Fuel Fact

Thin people can still have too much fat around their organs. Thin people who eat too much fat can have more fat around their hearts and livers than Japanese sumo wrestlers!

Fast foods, such as fries, often have lots of unhealthy trans fats.

# Functional Foods

Most food is good for us, even some fats and oils. Some foods are especially good for us. They not only give us nutrients, but also clean waste from the body and may relieve disease. These are called "functional foods."

## Functional Fats and Oils

Functional fats and oils are mainly polyunsaturated fats, rich in omega-3 fatty acids. When people do not eat enough omega-3 fatty acids they are more at risk of some diseases. These include attention deficit/hyperactivity disorder (ADHD), inflammatory bowel disease, and heart disease.

## Making Essential Fats

The body can make all its essential fats from omega-6 and omega-3 fatty acids. These two fatty acids make most of the fats in cell membranes and the special fat in our brains.

Choosing healthy oils can give people extra nutrients for good health.

# Choosing Functional Foods for Health

Choosing functional fats and oils can be good for our health. People can choose foods that are high in essential fatty acids. Foods with healthy fats include fish, soybeans, and olives.

## Fish

Omega-3 fatty acids from fish improve mental function and eyesight. They also reduce heart disease and may reduce ADHD.

## Soybean Oil

Lysine is a protein in soybeans and soybean oil. It promotes healing and may reduce cold sores. Omega-3 fatty acids from soybeans reduce **cholesterol** and fats in the bloodstream, so blood circulates easily.

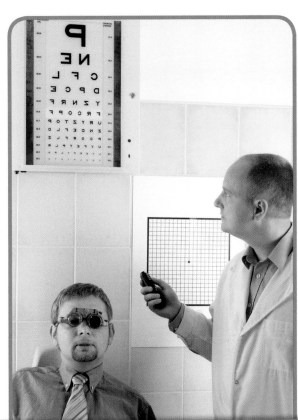

Omega-3 fatty acids can improve a person's eyesight, which can be checked by an optometrist.

Olives are crushed to produce olive oil, which can help carry lycopene around the body.

*Body Fuel Health Tips*

Two ingredients in Bolognese sauce are olive oil and tomato paste. Tomatoes have a powerful antioxidant called lycopene that protects your cells from damage. Lycopene is transported in fats. Olive oil is a great transporter of lycopene. When you are making Bolognese sauce, use a good extra-virgin olive oil and tomato paste for a supercharge of antioxidants.

19

# Naturally Healthy Fats and Oils

The easiest way to be naturally healthy is to eat a balanced diet from across the food pyramid. People need fats and oils in small amounts.

## Fats and Oils in the Diet

Many people have too much fat in their diet. This is unhealthy because people can become overweight. This can damage the heart, arteries, and skeleton. Being very overweight is called obesity.

Lots of people try to reduce body fat by cutting out all the fats from their diets. However, this may mean people do not get all the fatty acids they need. Some fatty acids are needed for brain function and cell membrane health.

To reduce fat in the diet, people can replace saturated fats with smaller amounts of polyunsaturated and mono-unsaturated fats. This reduces the calories in the diet while providing the nutrients we need. Increasing exercise is also important, because exercise burns energy.

Small amounts of polyunsaturated fats, such as peanut oil, provide healthy nutrients.

**Fabulous Body Fuel Fact**

Two pounds (one kilogram) of body fat is the same size as a loaf of bread. So if you are 6 lb (3 kg) overweight it is like strapping three loaves of bread to your body!

## Obesity

When people are very overweight they are called obese. Overweight children are at risk for obesity.

Obese children can develop adult diseases, such as type 2 diabetes, high blood pressure, and high cholesterol.

## Healthy Diet and Exercise

Eating too much fat makes people overweight. Many fast foods, cakes, and pastries contain lots of saturated fats.

Overweight people can lose excess fat by exercising and reducing fatty foods in the diet. Fatty foods can be replaced with fresh fruits, vegetables, grains, soy products, and lean meats.

Getting plenty of exercise helps prevent obesity.

# Fats and Oils Around the World

People around the world get their daily supply of fats and oils from local produce. Fats and oils are found in dairy foods, meats, fish, grains, and plants such as palm trees.

### Tibet
The people of Tibet depend on milk from yaks for much of their daily fat intake. Yaks are large, humped animals, a bit like a long-haired bull. Butter made from yak's milk can be mixed into a cup of tea. This is called *tsampa* in Tibetan.

### Greece, Italy, and the Middle East
Olive oil is a popular cooking oil in Greece, Italy, and the Middle East. These countries have grown olive trees for thousands of years. People press the olives from the trees to obtain oil.

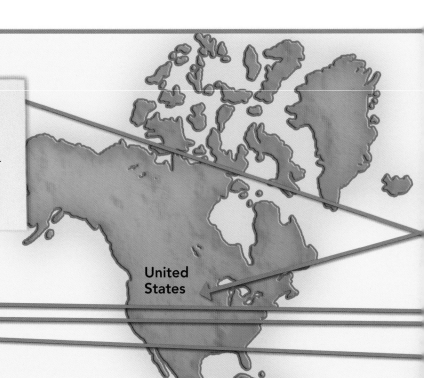

United States

### China
Many Chinese foods have a few drops of sesame oil for flavor. Sesame oil is a healthy oil made from sesame seeds. It is high in omega-3 fatty acids.

As you can see from this world map, people around the world eat different types of fats and oils.

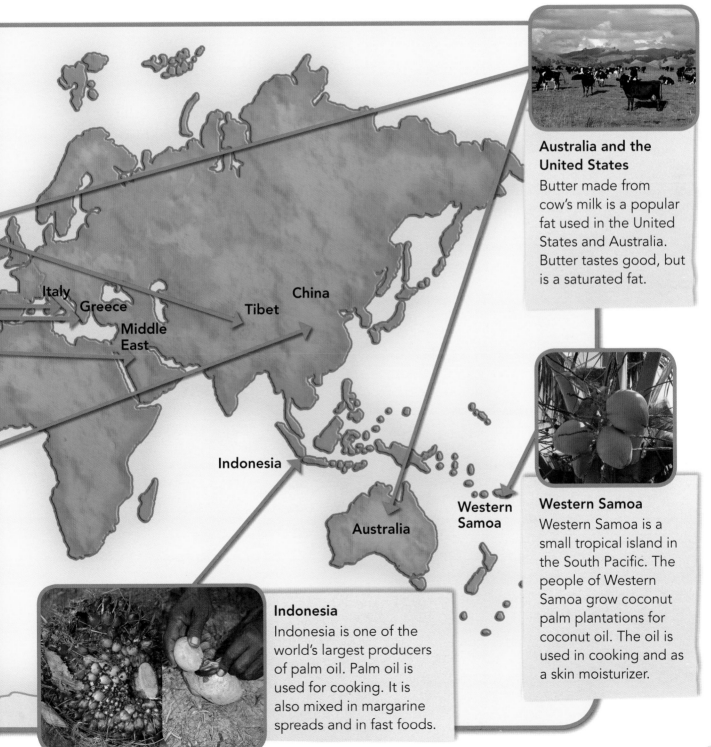

**Australia and the United States**
Butter made from cow's milk is a popular fat used in the United States and Australia. Butter tastes good, but is a saturated fat.

**Western Samoa**
Western Samoa is a small tropical island in the South Pacific. The people of Western Samoa grow coconut palm plantations for coconut oil. The oil is used in cooking and as a skin moisturizer.

**Indonesia**
Indonesia is one of the world's largest producers of palm oil. Palm oil is used for cooking. It is also mixed in margarine spreads and in fast foods.

Italy
Greece
Middle East
China
Tibet
Indonesia
Western Samoa
Australia

# Allergies and Intolerances to Fats and Oils

Food allergies and intolerances are reactions by our bodies to different foods. A food allergy occurs when the immune system reacts as if a food is dangerous. This reaction may cause itchy skin or make breathing difficult. A food intolerance is a negative chemical reaction in the body to the food. These reactions often cause similar symptoms to allergic reactions.

## Common Allergies and Intolerances

Allergies and intolerances specific to fats and oils are very uncommon. Allergies or intolerances to fats and oils are usually caused by the base ingredient of the oil. For example, someone who is allergic to peanuts will get a reaction from eating peanut oil. Some allergy-producing base ingredients of oils are:

- peanuts
- fish
- soybeans
- nuts.

Peanuts are a healthy food for most people, but can be dangerous for those with an allergy.

People who have allergies to these ingredients need to avoid dishes prepared with these oils.

### Peanuts

Peanuts can cause **anaphylaxis**, one of the most dangerous allergic reactions. Peanut oil will cause anaphylaxis in people with peanut allergies. If people have a severe allergic reaction, they must get medical help immediately.

Some people who are allergic to a food may get a lumpy, itchy rash called hives.

# What Oils Can I Eat if I Have Food Allergies?

There are many alternative fats and oils you can choose if you have an allergy. Polyunsaturated oils are more often made from allergy-producing foods, such as fish or nuts. Mono-unsaturated oils or saturated fats can replace polyunsaturated oils. However, mono-unsaturated oils are a much healthier choice than saturated fats.

Some substitute mono-unsaturated fats are olive oil, canola oil, and avocado oil. These are good substitutes for polyunsaturated fats because they may reduce cholesterol in the body.

Some substitute saturated fats are:

- butter
- lard
- coconut oil
- palm oil
- margarine made from palm oil.

These should only be eaten in very small amounts, because too much saturated fat is unhealthy.

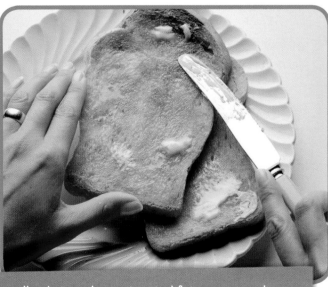

If you are allergic to polyunsaturated fats, you can choose other fats and oils, such as avocado oil or butter.

# Checking Food Labels for Fats and Oils

Food labels list the types of fats and oils and other ingredients used in packaged foods. This is so people can measure nutrient and energy levels in foods. It is best to choose foods with polyunsaturated fats.

## Allergies

Food labels can also be checked for allergy-producing ingredients. This is very important for people with food allergies.

**OLD FASHIONED NUTTY PEANUT BUTTER 16 OZ**

**Nutrition Facts**
Serv Size 2 Tbsp. (32g)
Servings About 14
Calories 210
Fat Cal 150
Percent Daily Values (DV) are based on a 2,000 calorie diet.

| Amount/Serving | % DV* | Amount/Serving | %DV* |
|---|---|---|---|
| **Total Fat** 16g | **25%** | Total Carb 6g | 2% |
| Sat Fat 2.5g | **12%** | Fiber 2g | 9% |
| Trans Fat 0g | | Sugars 1g | |
| **Cholest** 0mg | **0%** | Protein 8g | |
| **Sodium** 120mg | **5%** | | |

Vitamin A 0% • Vitamin C 0% • Calcium 0% • Iron 2%

INGREDIENTS: PEANUTS AND SALT.
THE J.M. SMUCKER COMPANY
ORRVILLE, OHIO 44667 U.S.A.
CALL FREE with Questions or Comments
1-800-9553 M–F 9am–7pm (EST).

27167

02

0  51500 05061

You can check a food label to see if the food contains any unhealthy trans fats.

**Nutrition Facts**
Serving Size 1/6 package (60g)
Servings Per Container 6

| Amount Per Serving | | Mix Prepared |
|---|---|---|
| Calories | 260 | 360 |
| Calories from Fat | 80 | 150 |

| | % Daily Value* | |
|---|---|---|
| **Total Fat** 9g* | 14% | 26% |
| Saturated Fat 3.5g | 18% | 30% |
| **Cholesterol** 0mg | 0% | 1% |
| **Sodium** 360mg | 15% | 20% |
| **Total Carbohydrate** 46g | 15% | 16% |
| Dietary Fiber 1g | 4% | 4% |
| Sugars 28g | | |
| **Protein** 2g | | |
| Vitamin A | 0% | 10% |
| Vitamin C | 0% | 0% |
| Calcium | 15% | 25% |
| Iron | 6% | 6% |

Food labels can tell you how many calories and how much fat the food contains.

# Checking Food Labels for Healthy Fats

Food labels make it easy for people to choose healthier types of foods. By reading food labels, people can compare ingredients and select healthier options.

## Comparing Food Labels

Food labels help people compare the fats in packaged foods. Some packaged foods may taste similar, but have different fats. Foods with polyunsaturated or mono-unsaturated fats are healthier than foods with saturated fats. Choose foods with:

- less fat (in total)
- mono-unsaturated fats
- polyunsaturated fats
- no trans fats (often called hydrogenated oils).

## Checking for Allergens

Food labels can help people avoid foods to which they may be allergic. If you have an allergy, check food labels for these fats and oils:

- peanuts
- soybeans
- fish or seafood
- nuts.

### Body Fuel Health Tips

Some people suffer from a nut, seed, or seafood allergy. They need to read the ingredients list of every oil to find its true source. Mono-unsaturated oil is likely to be a safer choice than polyunsaturated oil.

People can use the information on food labels to choose healthier foods when shopping.

# Cooking Class

**Ask an adult to help you.**

Cooking low-fat meals is easy. People can broil foods instead of frying, or foods can be steamed. Follow these recipes for Sesame Stir-fried Vegetables and Steamed Chicken and Ginger Soy Packets to get:

- protein for cell renewal
- carbohydrate for energy
- polyunsaturated oils for healthy skin and cell membranes
- vitamins and minerals for healthy chemical reactions in the body.

## Sesame Stir-fried Vegetables

**Servings** Four
**Preparation time** 15 minutes
**Cooking time** 5 minutes

### Ingredients

2 green onions

1 tablespoon polyunsaturated oil

1/4 teaspoon sesame oil

1/2 bok choy, chopped

1 red pepper, sliced into strips

1/2 can (about 20) baby corn, chopped

1 cup whole, fresh snow peas

3 garlic cloves, chopped finely

### Preparation

1. Chop the green onions into 1-inch (3-centimeter) pieces.

2. Place the oils into a wok or large frying pan. Fry the bok choy, peppers, baby corn, snow peas, and garlic over high heat for about 5 minutes, stirring quickly.

green onions

red pepper

polyunsaturated oil

baby corn

sesame oil

snow peas

bok choy

garlic cloves

# Steamed Chicken and Ginger Soy Packets

**Servings**   Four
**Preparation time**   45 minutes
**Cooking time**   30 minutes

## Ingredients

1 teaspoon sugar

2 tablespoons soy sauce

1/2 cup chicken stock

1 teaspoon lemon juice

1-inch (2-centimeter) piece of ginger root,
    peeled and roughly chopped

2 skinless chicken breasts, halved

4 sheets of aluminum foil 12 inches (30 centimeters) square

## Preparation

1. Preheat the oven to 350 degrees Fahrenheit
    (180 degrees Celsius).

2. Mix the sugar, soy sauce, chicken stock,
    lemon juice, and ginger in a bowl.

3. Marinate chicken breasts in this mixture
    for 30 minutes.

4. Place the sheets of foil in a baking dish.

5. Place the marinated chicken on the foil and spoon the
    remaining sauce over the chicken.

6. Fold the foil into packets and place in the oven for about
    30 minutes, or until cooked.

## Serving

Serve with brown rice. Lay the steamed chicken and sauce over
the rice. Arrange the stir-fried vegetables around the chicken for a
delicious and healthy meal.

sugar

soy sauce

chicken stock

lemon juice

ginger root

chicken breasts

aluminum foil

# Fueling the Body with Healthy Fats and Oils

People need to eat some fats and oils to fuel the body and maintain good health. Fats give people healthy brain function and make skin waterproof. They carry vitamins and hormones throughout the body, keep us warm, and protect our organs. However, people need to eat small amounts of fats and be careful which fats they choose.

Fatty fast foods contain unhealthy trans fats and saturated fats. These fats can cause diabetes, heart disease, and cancer. People can improve their health and prevent diseases by changing the fats and oils they eat.

Remember always to choose polyunsaturated or mono-unsaturated fats. These are filled with essential omega-3 and omega-6 fatty acids. Limit saturated fats and make sure to read food labels so you can choose the healthiest fats. Eating the right fats and oils in the right amounts will give you body fuel for a healthy body.

A balanced diet of fresh, healthy foods contains the right amounts of fats for terrific body fuel.

# Glossary

| | |
|---|---|
| **anaphylaxis** | a very strong allergic reaction that can quickly cause death if not treated |
| **antioxidant** | a chemical that protects cells from damage |
| **balanced diet** | a mix of different foods that provides the right amount of nutrients for the body |
| **bolus** | a small ball of chewed food |
| **cells** | microscopic structures that combine to make up all the bones, muscles, and other parts of the body |
| **chemical reactions** | processes by which substances are changed into other substances |
| **cholesterol** | a fat that is needed by the body, but which causes disease if too much is taken in |
| **churned** | stirred very quickly |
| **clotting** | hardening to form a lump, such as a scab |
| **digestive enzymes** | proteins that speed up the chemical reactions involved in the digestion of food |
| **evacuation** | removal from the body |
| **fat-soluble vitamins** | vitamins that are transported in fat |
| **feces** | solid waste that is evacuated from the body |
| **hormones** | substances made in cells that help control the body's functions |
| **hydrogenated** | has had the gas hydrogen added |
| **immune system** | the body system that fights infections |
| **internal organs** | parts inside the body that perform a function, such as the heart or lungs |
| **lymphatic system** | a network of vessels, similar to blood vessels, that transports fats and is part of the immune system |
| **nutrients** | substances that provide energy when eaten |
| **rectum** | the end of the large intestine, where feces are stored before evacuation |
| **saliva** | the fluid in the mouth that helps digest food |
| **villi** | small, fingerlike bumps on the inside wall of the small intestine |

# Index